GO FACTS **HEALTHY BODIES**

Staying Safe

Liz Flaherty

A & C BLACK • LONDON

Staying Safe

contents

© 2007 Blake Publishing
Additional material © A & C Black Publishers Ltd 2009

First published in Australia by Blake Education Pty Ltd.

This edition published in the United Kingdom in 2009 by
A & C Black Publishers Ltd, 36 Soho Square, London, W1D 3QY.
www.acblack.com

Hardback edition
ISBN 978-1-4081-1222-9

Paperback edition
ISBN 978-1-4081-1220-5

A CIP record for this book is available from the British Library.

Written by Liz Flaherty
Publisher: Katy Pike
Editor: Mark Stafford
Design and layout by The Modern Art Production Group.

Image credits: p11 top—© Newspix/Michael Perini; p21 top, bottom right—Liz Flaherty

Printed in China by WKT Company Ltd.

This book is produced using paper that is made from wood grown in managed
sustainable forests. It is natural, renewable and recyclable. The logging and
manufacturing processes conform to the environmental regulations of the country
of origin.

What is Safety?

Every environment has potential hazards. By recognising the hazards, it is often possible to avoid danger and harm.

People make decisions every day that keep them safe. Most people naturally check for traffic before crossing a road, or keep away from the edge of a cliff.

Sometimes it is necessary to think more carefully about potential hazards. For example, rock fishing is a dangerous sport because the ocean is unpredictable. People can be washed out to sea. To make it less dangerous, fishermen watch their fishing spot for at least 30 minutes before beginning to fish, to check the wave conditions.

Your body gives warning signals when there is danger. Your palms sweat and your heart beats faster. Responding to danger in a calm and thoughtful way can minimise risk.

First to the rescue

First aid is immediate treatment for someone who is ill or injured, before a doctor has the chance to help. Anyone can learn first aid for treating minor injuries, such as cuts, sprains and stings.

The St John Ambulance organisation provides first aid at public events. More than 124 000 casualties are treated by St John Ambulance volunteers in the UK each year.

DID YOU KNOW?
Over 600 people drown every year in the UK.

4

Lifeguards are trained in rescue techniques and first aid.

A first aid kit should include bandages, dressings, scissors, antiseptic and basic medicines.

Rock fishermen should wear shoes with **rubber soles** that grip slippery rocks.

Signs warn people of hazards.

CAUTION
Wet Floor

Cuidado
Piso Mojado

Road Safety

On average, eight people are killed every day on British roads.

Cars can kill

Being a safe pedestrian means being visible and crossing roads at the safest locations – traffic lights, pedestrian crossings and away from parked cars.

Inside a car, seatbelts and airbags save lives. Wearing a seatbelt was made compulsory in the UK in 1983. Drivers and passengers who don't wear a seatbelt are 18 times more likely to be killed in a road accident than those wearing a seatbelt.

On your bike

On the road, bicycles are considered vehicles. Cyclists have a right to use the road, but they must obey road rules.

Some roads have lanes for cyclists. These reduce the chance of accidents between cars and bicycles, especially in busy city streets.

Cyclists can be difficult to see. They should wear bright or light-coloured clothing, and keep in a straight line one metre out from the gutter and parked cars. Cyclists should constantly scan the environment for pedestrians and other vehicles.

Bicycle helmets save lives and reduce the risk of head injuries. Helmets have a foam shell which absorbs any impact to the head during an accident.

GO FACT!

DID YOU KNOW?

The main cause of injury and death in a car crash is when the driver and passengers are thrown around inside the car. At 30 miles per hour this is like falling from the top of a three-storey building. Seatbelts prevent this and reduce the risk of injury and death.

About 80 per cent of cyclists admitted to hospital did not collide with another vehicle — they lost control of their bicycles.

When riding with friends, each rider should make their own decisions about road safety.

More than half the injuries that cause death for 10 – 14 year olds are due to road accidents.

Airbags halve the chance of suffering a serious head injury in an accident.

Burns

Burns affect the surface of the skin and may damage deep tissues. Severe burns can lead to shock, infection and death.

Types of burns

There are three types of burn injuries.

first degree burn	The epidermis (outer layer of skin) is burned. Heals well after being cooled with water.
second degree burn	The epidermis is burned and blisters. Needs medical treatment.
third degree burn	All layers of the skin are burned. Nerves, tissue and muscles are damaged. Needs urgent medical treatment.

The deeper the burn and the greater body area it covers, the greater the risk to the patient. Burnt airways can make breathing difficult.

Treating burns

It is important to treat all burns quickly, to reduce pain and prevent scarring. Treatment aims to stop the burning, relieve pain and swelling, and minimise the risk of infection.

First aid for a burn:

1 Run cold water over the burn for at least 20 minutes.

2 Remove any jewellery, belts or tight clothing near the burn.

3 Cover the burn with a clean dressing.

4 Assess whether further treatment is needed.

If the body cannot heal a burn itself, doctors may repair the burn with a skin **graft**. Skin is removed from an area that is usually clothed, such as the thigh. It is laid over the wound, and stitched or stapled into position.

It takes five minutes for water at 50° Celsius to cause a third degree burn. It takes just one second at 60° Celsius to cause the same burn.

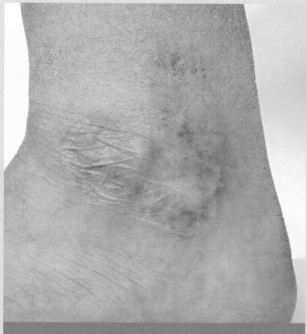

Deep burns may not be as painful as surface burns because they destroy nerve endings.

Smoke alarms provide an early warning of a home fire.

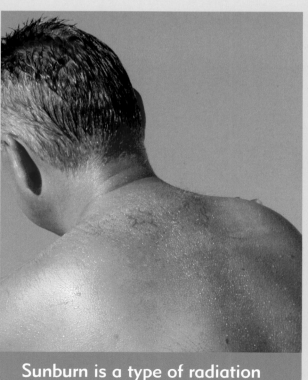

Sunburn is a type of radiation burn.

Poisoning and Bites

Poisons are substances which enter the bloodstream and cause illness and sometimes death. Venoms are poisons produced by animals or plants.

Poison

Many household products, such as medicines, pesticides and cleaning supplies, are poisonous. Young children are most at risk from poisoning, so such products should be locked out of reach and sight.

The symptoms of poisoning vary, depending on the poison and how much is swallowed. They may include vomiting, stomach pain and drowsiness.

Bites and stings

Australia has some of the world's most poisonous creatures. About 3 000 people are bitten by snakes every year.

However, in the UK, there is only one kind of poisonous snake, the viper. The last fatality from a snake bite in the UK was in 1975.

Most bites can be avoided by simply leaving dangerous animals alone.

To treat a snake bite in the past, the venom was sucked out of the victim. Whoever sucked out the poison then vomited – this often caused more damage than the bite! The correct treatment for a snake bite is to start bandaging the area near the bite and then wind the bandage firmly along the full length of the limb. The bite victim should remain very still to stop the venom moving through the body.

The bluebottle, or Portuguese Man O' War, delivers a painful sting – even if it is dead.

The Sydney funnel web spider has killed 13 people in and around Sydney. Its fangs are large and powerful enough to puncture a fingernail. Antivenom, a drug that cancels the effect of venom, has been available for this species since 1980. Since the introduction of antivenoms, there have been no recorded deaths in Australia from spider bites.

DID YOU KNOW?
A male platypus has poisonous spurs on the back of its legs. Pain from an attack can last for days or weeks.

Are these pills or lollies?* Many medicines look like lollies or chewing gum. They should always be kept out of children's reach.

*They are pills.

11

It's an Emergency!

An ambulance service provides care at the scene of a medical emergency and on the way to hospital.

Calling for help

Dial 999 to contact emergency services. This is a free call from any phone, even a pay-as-you-go mobile phone.

Try to stay calm and speak slowly. An operator asks which service is needed – ambulance, police or fire. Ask for ambulance. Your call is connected to the ambulance operations centre. An operator asks a standard set of questions, which include:

- What is the exact location of the emergency?
- What is the phone number you're calling from?
- What is the problem? Tell me exactly what happened.
- Is the person **conscious**?
- Is the person breathing?

Help on the way

The operator decides how urgent the emergency is, based on these answers. He or she contacts an ambulance and tells the **paramedics** about the emergency.

While the ambulance is on the way, it is important to stay on the phone – the operator may have instructions or more questions.

When the ambulance arrives, the paramedics assess the situation and continue any treatment that has begun. If necessary, they take the person to a hospital.

GO FACT!
ON THE SCENE
75 per cent of ambulances arrive at an accident within eight minutes of the emergency call.

Lights and sirens are only used if the patient's condition is life-threatening or getting worse quickly.

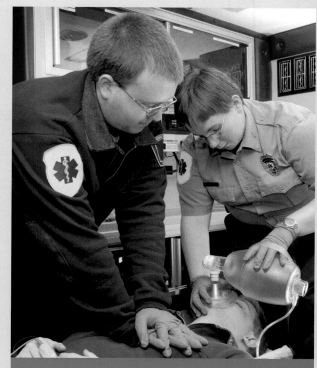

Paramedics usually work in pairs.

An air ambulance is used to transport critically ill patients and reach emergencies in remote areas.

'Ambulance' is often printed backwards on the vehicle, so that a driver in front can read it correctly through a rear-view mirror — and then get out of the way!

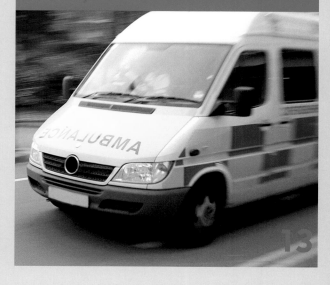

Electrical Shock

The human body is a good conductor of electricity.

Electricity surges through the body during an electrical shock. It burns the skin and internal tissues, especially where it enters and leaves the body. Electricity can also make the heart stop or beat irregularly.

Electrical shock can occur by touching power lines, faulty appliances and damaged cables. It is also caused by lightning, and by electrical appliances touching water.

To use electricity safely, check that plugs and cords are in good condition. Do not use anything electrical in a wet place, such as in the bathroom or around a pool. Never touch anything electrical with wet hands.

Never overload a plug socket.

A licensed electrician should do all electrical work around the house. A safety switch between a plug socket and an appliance can detect if the appliance is faulty. If an electrical shock is about to occur, the switch shuts down electricity in $\frac{1}{30\,000}$ of a second.

Treating a shock

If you are with someone who receives an electrical shock, act quickly. Turn off the power supply. DO NOT touch the person until the power supply is turned off. Start **resuscitation** if the person has stopped breathing. Dial 999 for an ambulance.

GO FACT!
MOST STRIKES

Ex-park ranger Roy C. Sullivan was struck by lightning seven times and survived.

Electricians use fibreglass or wooden ladders, because metal ladders conduct electricity.

Old electrical wiring can be dangerous. An electrical fault, which could have started a fire, melted this plug.

Safety covers prevent young children sticking things in plug sockets.

Indoors is the safest place to be during an electrical storm.

Body Fluids

Blood and other body fluids can carry disease. People can become infected by not handling body fluids safely.

Body fluids include blood, saliva, urine, **semen** and **faeces**. They can carry hepatitis (a virus that attacks the liver), HIV (the virus that can lead to **AIDS**) and bacterial infections.

A person can pass disease to another person if body fluids pass through the membranes of the mouth and eyes, or if they splash onto open cuts. Disease can also be passed on by **contaminated** equipment and unclean work areas.

At risk

Some people are at risk of infection from body fluids because of the work they do. Doctors, nurses and research scientists handle body fluids every day. They wear masks, glasses and gloves for protection. They may also be **vaccinated** against hepatitis.

They always wash their hands thoroughly with soap and water before and after examining a patient and after handling body fluids. Disposable needles, used in medicine and body piercing, are used once only.

The rules of most contact sports say that if an injured player is bleeding, he or she must leave the game until the bleeding stops. This allows the injured player to be treated, but also protects other players from contact with blood.

GO FACT!
DID YOU KNOW?
The UK needs more than two million blood donations every year to meet the hospitals' blood requirements.

16

Paramedics always wear gloves when they treat an injured person.

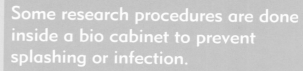

Some research procedures are done inside a bio cabinet to prevent splashing or infection.

It takes at least 20 seconds to wash your hands properly.

Needles and blades that have touched body fluids are put in a sealed sharps container.

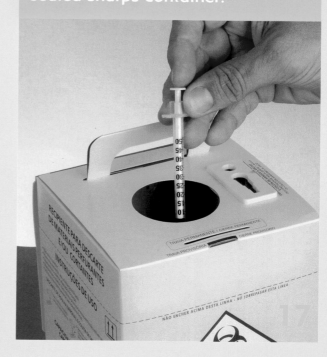

What is Shock?

What does it mean when somebody 'goes into shock'?

The human body needs oxygen. Blood carries oxygen to all the body's organs. The body goes into shock if its organs don't get oxygen.

There are many causes of shock. Heart attacks and sudden, massive blood loss can stop blood from reaching organs.

Symptoms of shock

In the early stages of shock, the patient's heart rate quickens. The skin becomes cold and clammy. It may become pale blue-grey – especially around the lips.

Breathing becomes rapid and shallow, and the patient may feel weak and dizzy. Other symptoms include **nausea**, thirst and a weak **pulse**.

Severe shock may lead to unconsciousness and death.

Dangerous allergies

A special type of shock is called anaphylactic shock. It is a severe allergic reaction, usually to peanuts, seafood, insect stings or medicines.

Symptoms include difficulty in breathing and talking, which is caused by swelling in the throat. Young children become pale and weak.

Anaphylactic shock needs urgent medical attention because it can kill in seconds. The emergency treatment is an injection of adrenaline, which is a chemical produced by the body that makes the heart beat faster. People who know they are allergic to certain foods often carry adrenaline with them.

GO FACT!
DID YOU KNOW?

About one in 20 children and one in 100 adults have food allergies.

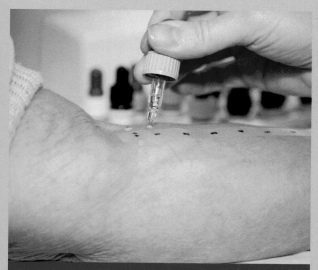

A skin allergy test can detect a food allergy. The skin is pricked with a needle and a drop of **allergen** is placed on the skin. If a person is allergic, a small bump like a mosquito bite appears.

Many schools ban nuts and peanut butter to protect children who have food allergies.

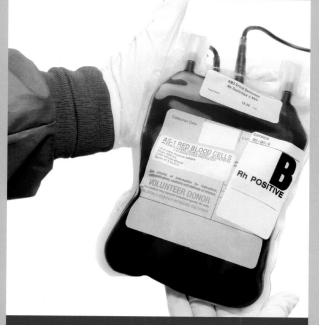

A transfusion replaces blood if more than 20 per cent of normal volume is lost.

This device gives an automatic injection of adrenaline when jabbed into the thigh.

Survival Swimming

All swimming places – pools, rivers, dams and the surf – have hazards. Survival swimming is a group of skills to help survive an emergency in the water.

Survival swimming includes the ability, while fully dressed, to swim, **scull** and tread water. Survival swimmers can also swim underwater on their backs, and use aids, such as rope, to assist in a rescue.

Check for hazards

Many people are seriously injured jumping or diving into water that is too shallow. Check out any swimming spot before jumping or diving in. Do this by getting into the water to check the depth. Also, make sure the area is clear of rocks, snags, sandbanks and weeds.

Rip tides

A rip is a strong ocean current heading away from shore. It can travel at several metres per second and drag swimmers hundreds of metres offshore. People often try to swim against the rip, then become exhausted and drown. Rip tides are the most common cause of all sea rescues.

Remember the three Rs if you are caught in a rip:

- RELAX – float or swim with the current, not against it
- RAISE – one arm to signal for help
- RESCUE – float and wait for help.

DID YOU KNOW?
Every year over 18 000 people are rescued from UK beaches by trained lifeguards.

Before going boating, check the weather conditions and wear a personal flotation device.

Always check safety signs before entering the water.

GELLIBRAND RIVER

Swimming Not Recommended

Strong Currents

Submerged Rocks

Unstable Cliffs Keep Clear

Unpatrolled Area

Parks Victoria advise that this beach is not patrolled by Lifesavers. The nearest patrolled beach is located at the Port Campbell Foreshore - Distance 18km. Port Campbell Foreshore is patrolled only when the red and yellow flags are displayed by Lifesavers.

DOGS PROHIBITED   FIRES PROHIBITED   CAMPING PROHIBITED   MOTORBIKES PROHIBITED   COLLECTION PROHIBITED

PARK INFORMATION 13 1963   Parks

If there is a boating accident, stay with the boat, hold onto any floating object and huddle with other people.

Resuscitation

In an emergency, the brain can only survive for three to four minutes without the blood's oxygen. Resuscitation restores breathing and gets the heart pumping again.

The ABC of resuscitation describes how an unconscious person is helped.

A is for airway

Open the airway and check for blockages. Watch the chest to see if it rises and falls. Listen for breathing sounds.

B is for breathing

If the patient is not breathing, start mouth-to-mouth resuscitation. Also called expired air resuscitation, this involves forcing air into the patient's lungs.

C is for circulation

Check for a pulse. The easiest place to check is on the neck, next to the patient's **Adam's apple**. If there is no pulse, cardiopulmonary resuscitation (CPR) is started. CPR combines mouth-to-mouth resuscitation with pushes on the chest. The pushes massage the heart and keep **oxygenated** blood flowing to the brain and other organs.

Learn to save

Resuscitation is a valuable skill. First aid courses teach people how to resuscitate someone safely. If not performed properly, CPR can cause broken ribs and damaged lungs. **NEVER** practise on a person who does not need it!

GO FACT!

DID YOU KNOW?

The heart pumps more the 250 million litres of blood in an average lifetime.

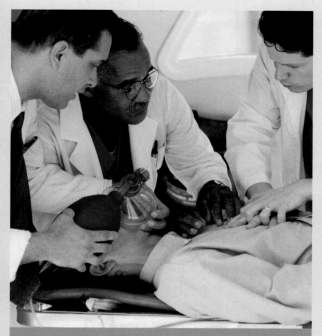

CPR is less likely to save a life in reality than it does in television medical dramas.

Exhaled air contains about 15 per cent oxygen, which is enough to help an unconscious person.

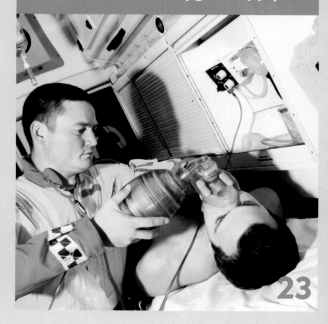

A BVM (bag-valve-mask) is often used by paramedics for expired air resuscitation. It can also be connected to an oxygen supply.

People use dummies to practise resuscitation.

23

EMERGENCY DEFIBRILLATOR

Heart Starters

Emergency workers may use a defibrillator to make a heart pump blood.

A cardiac arrest is when the heart stops pumping blood. It may occur due to heart disease, electric shock, drug overdose or severe blood loss. Sometimes, the heart quivers like jelly after a cardiac arrest, rather than lying still. The heart's muscle fibres are contracting, but not in a coordinated way, so the heart cannot pump blood.

Paddles

A defibrillator is a machine designed to make the heart beat normally. It consists of metal paddles, or **electrodes**, that are held against the skin of the patient near the heart.

The defibrillator gives an electrical shock to the heart. Electricity passes from one paddle, through the skin and the heart, and out of the other paddle. The shock stops the action of individual muscle fibres and allows the normal heartbeat to start again.

Automatic version

Many ambulances carry a defibrillator, and all hospital emergency wards have them. An automated defibrillator monitors a heart's rhythm and automatically delivers an electric shock if required. People who are at risk of having a cardiac arrest may have a small, battery-powered defibrillator **implanted** in their chests. This is called a pacemaker.

GO FACT!
DID YOU KNOW?
Defibrillation can improve a patient's chance of survival to well over 50 per cent if used within three minutes of a cardiac arrest.

The paddles are insulated to protect the operator from electrical shock.

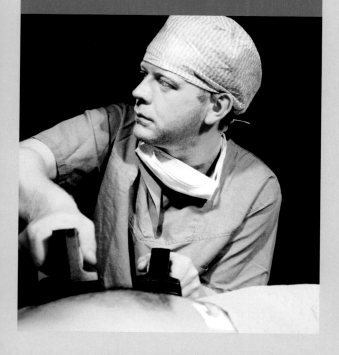

Most cardiac arrests occur outside of hospital, so automated defibrillators are installed in public places.

A defibrillator's shock lasts only 4 – 12 milliseconds.

In a hospital, a trolley that contains a defibrillator and drugs to treat a cardiac arrest is called a crash cart.

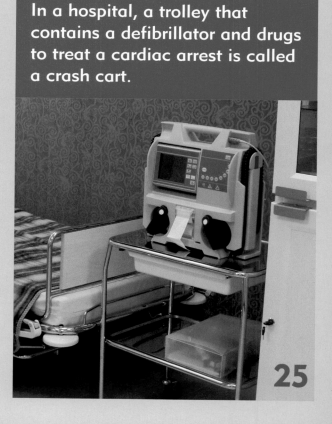

Home Safety Check

Most accidents happen around the home. How safe is your home?

Complete this home safety check and see how it rates.

What to do:

1 Photocopy the table opposite.

2 Check your home, room by room, and answer 'yes' or 'no' for each question.

3 Working with an adult, take action to improve safety where needed and then tick 'action taken'.

	yes	no	action taken
General			
Do you have working smoke alarms?			
Are electrical cords out of sight and reach of children?			
Are all curtain and blind cords out of reach of children?			
Is top-heavy furniture (bookshelves, televisions, etc.) secure and stable?			
Are balcony railings free of footholds?			
Is there a first aid kit in the house?			
Do you have the phone number for NHS Direct and other emergency services beside every phone?			
Kitchen			
Is there a fire blanket or fire extinguisher nearby?			
Are cleaning products out of reach?			
Are knives out of reach?			
Are appliances and wires out of reach?			
Living room			
Are heaters clear of curtains and furniture?			
Are safety plugs in unused power sockets?			
Are sharp edges of furniture covered?			
Laundry			
Are cleaning products out of reach and locked away?			
Have old and unused medicines and poisons been thrown away?			
Bathroom			
Are razors and hair dryers out of reach?			
Is there a bath mat to prevent slipping?			
Are medicines out of reach and locked away?			
Bedroom			
Are bunk beds fitted with a safety rail at least 160 mm above the mattress?			
Garage/shed and outside			
Are all chemicals (paints, gardening products, etc.) out of reach and locked away?			
If you have a pool or spa, is it surrounded by a 1.2 m high fence with a self-closing and self-latching gate?			
Is there a CPR poster near the pool/spa?			

Staying Safe

Who's responsible for your safety?

When we're very young, our parents look after our needs and keep us safe. As we grow older, we become responsible for our actions and our own safety.

It's your choice

Peer groups are groups of friends who are all about the same age. They help us become independent and learn to live in the world of our own age group.

Pressure from a peer group can sometimes lead us into doing things we would not normally do. Sometimes peers are right, sometimes they are wrong. The best way to keep safe – and keep the respect of your friends and yourself – is to make your own decisions about your safety.

Your safety situation

You must look at situations and decide how safe they are. Think of a traffic light.

When a traffic light is green, it is safe to proceed. If the light is yellow, you must be careful and prepare to stop. If the light turns red, it's time to stop.

Use the same lights to know when you are safe, need to use caution, or should stop because there is danger. It is important to teach yourself to recognise different situations, and be aware when your safety situation changes from green to yellow or to red.

Parents and teachers can always guide you, but you are responsible for yourself and the choices you make.

DID YOU KNOW?
Alcohol and other drugs affect a person's ability to make safe decisions. About one-third of pedestrians killed in the UK have a blood alcohol reading higher than the legal limit.

To make safe decisions on the road, cyclists need to know the road rules. You'll find the answers to these quiz questions on page 32.

True or false?

1 You must stop at red traffic lights and stop signs.

2 You may ride two abreast (ie, beside another cyclist) on a road.

3 It's OK to ride across a pedestrian crossing if you warn pedestrians with your bell.

4 It is safe to ride at night without lights, as long as you keep to quiet roads and your bike has reflectors.

5 You must always wear a helmet.

6 If you've got good balance, it's OK to ride with only one hand on the handle bars.

7 You don't need to use a hand signal if you are turning right.

8 You may carry someone else on your bike if they wear a helmet.

9 Your bike must have a working bell.

10 You can hang on to another vehicle while riding your bike, as long as you don't break the speed limit.

Glossary

Adam's apple (noun) the part of the throat that sticks out and moves up and down during speech and swallowing

AIDS (noun) stands for Acquired Immune Deficiency Syndrome; a disease caused by a virus that destroys the immune system

allergen (noun) a substance which can cause an allergy, but which is harmless to most people

conscious (adjective) awake, thinking and aware of what is happening

contaminated (adjective) spoilt or impure because of contact with something unclean

electrode (noun) a conductor through which electricity enters or leaves something

faeces (noun) solid waste remaining after food has been digested

graft (noun) a piece of healthy skin or bone cut from one part of a person's body and used to repair a damaged part; a piece cut from a living plant and fixed to another plant

implant (verb) to insert an organ, group of cells, or device into the body

membrane (noun) a thin layer of tissue that covers or connects parts of the body

nausea (noun) a feeling that you are going to vomit

oxygenated (adjective) supplied with oxygen

paramedic (noun) a person who is trained to do medical work, especially in an emergency, but who is not a doctor or nurse

pulse (noun) the regular throbbing of the arteries caused by the heart beating

resuscitation (noun) techniques to return someone to life or consciousness

scull (verb) to swim while floating on the front or the back, with the arms close to the body, moving only the wrists

semen (noun) a whitish liquid containing sperm produced by the sex organs of men and some male animals

vaccinated (verb) to have been given a substance which contains a safe form of a virus or bacterium, in order to be protected from getting the disease which the virus or bacterium causes

Index

Answers to quiz on page 30:

1. true 2. true 3. false 4. false 5. true
6. false 7. false 8. false 9. true 10. false